Ripples In The Sand

Tonia Teresa Healey

PITTSBURGH, PENNSYLVANIA 15238

The contents of this work including, but not limited to, the accuracy of events, people, and places depicted; opinions expressed; permission to use previously published materials included; and any advice given or actions advocated are solely the responsibility of the author, who assumes all liability for said work and indemnifies the publisher against any claims stemming from publication of the work.

RoseDog Books
585 Alpha Drive
Suite 103
Pittsburgh, PA 15238
Visit our website at *www.rosedogbookstore.com*

ISBN: 978-1-6442-6797-4
eISBN: 978-1-6442-6820-9

Every block of stone has a statue inside it

And it is the task of the sculptor to discover it.

Michelangelo

This is a Memoir of discovery, come follow me..

Table of Contents

Searching for Answers

This book is dedicated to my family, friends and loved ones
that have left me. It spans many years and many emotions.

Searching for answers, trying to help those who reach out to me,
my life has been full of love, happiness and some sorrow.
I am assembling this book of poems for all to hold as a memory.

Clarification

The turbulent oceans of my mind erupt,
demanding entrance through closed doors

A noble need now freed
surges to clarify these currents.

Interim caves of isolation
contain reservoirs of energy necessary
for new freedoms
and
to stand breathing above
the draining undertow.

Dreams are made in the mind, thinking of what we want, or have, or want to have. These poems are from those dreams. These poems are the reality of our experiences in life. They are also memories of love and intimate moments. They are the second part of my journey.

I envisioned the sculpture within the stone,

I cleared away the sand, and began the journey of life.

I would have been alone on this journey had it not been for my boys but with them beside me, we traveled on as "three against the world".

Working as a Poetry Therapist at RIH for the next ten years, I grew and also did my boys. They grew into amazing men and I grew into a great poet and therapist. I met many interesting people and had many life changing events. Some of these poems reflect those moments. Others are from personal experiences.

Closure

The summer of my 45th year,
the world I had shut out
still had never denied my
presence. The doors were open,
I was not ready. I told no one.
I was not sad, but said,
"God, I believe in a miracle,
a kind of grace that plays
in a cathedral. My existence
will be marked and remembered,
as the blush of my hand will
be a souvenir for my children.

Before I knew you, before
I knew myself, we were walking
in streets etched in dreams.
We were holding hands. I saw
what you saw and followed
you into your dream.
Your past was my history,
and no one knew.

We stood on an empty
beach, the wind pulling the words
out of our mouths and eating them.
Unable to speak, we walked

together through dunes, laying
our brown bodies on the white sand.

We loved as though the world
did not exist. Your tongue
touched my skin; nipples puckered
with wanting, we lay in the warm sand
and tossed together in the flaming surf.
How will we claim the roaring wind
or know the depth of sea?
How will we choose to walk from here
and find our destiny

Oh, Say Can You See

Written in the 80's..

Refrain:

"Rest quietly in your bed tonight;
all's peace throughout the land.
Though some things may not seem just right,
He's got the upper hand."

The year is two thousand twenty.
Man has no need for man.
A cell will make a new baby.
Science has fixed the Plan.

(Repeat refrain)

Our children live so happily
Within Skinner's design;
Rewards or pain, full stimuli,
keeps them all in line.

(Repeat refrain)

How carefree is our perfect life,
A verdant paradise;
Commitment to our sovereign lord
Has opened up our eyes.

(Repeat refrain)

We've no more malformations
        or inherited disease.
We've no more racial problems.
        Euthanasia is a breeze!

(Repeat refrain)

Utopia is here at last,
        All hail the sovereign lord.
With all things new and beautiful,
        How come we're all so bored?

While I was walking with a friend at Situate Reservoir in Rhode Island I thought about the beauty I saw and how it taught about love.

Lesson of Love

I have come to this forest
that time has undressed
and lain it's canopy on the
rich, dark floor. I have come
to ask what time has done
and how it could be forgiven.

Once full-bloomed trees now
stand skeletons against orange
sky, and ducklings cuddle closer
to downy warmth. The osprey fills
its wing to feed its young. My
hands touch the earth and know.

I learn from the survivors—
the water, the wind, the earth,
and the rain; they too come back
year after year. Perennial
bed fellows are the clover, lions tooth,
and star thistle, they thrive in the light,
and they cast a small shadow,

they nurture, but then they
withe in green shade.

How did I know?
The austere beauty of this place
was itself the answer.

Another lesson learned from the forest and the sea.

Dependent Parallel

When the white fog burns from the
Mountaintop, the cosmos is revealed.
Smoke spirals from points of fir trees
into everlasting light.

Cold sea is the other half of this bond
intense, eternal. Salt feeding us,
feeding the snow-capped mountain.

We walk into the ocean at brightest noon;
our bodies taste of salt, sparkle of gold.

Afterwards, we wrap ourselves in blankets
of mist and kiss the salt from our lips.
We give in to each other,
but not into each other's keeping.

Poems of Love

Then there are poems about love that don't need a story because it was once a story.

Awakening

Exquisite is your mouth
holding mine, tracing a jagged
path across my body—
eyes, chin, nipple puckers
beneath your kiss.
Soft, round tummy delights
as tongue tickles down
into the curly mound.
My essence flows
into you,
and you fill me.

The shadows that dressed me
in darkness at once banished.
And I, in innocent nakedness,
am no longer afraid.

I reach for daybreak,
touching stars,
holding your body,
giving, feeding the flame,
burning your flesh into mine.

Breaking Through

On the day that the wall fell,
the black rain beat on the window.
We lay like Siamese, spine to spine,
in exhausted sleep. Dream broken by alarm,
my body turned flat to the bed. Your arm
came around and held me quietly; belonging
only to this moment, time held itself.
"The room is so cold with rain," I said,
and you, with your flowers and your kisses,
said prayers to my breasts and my eyes.
You are the great power of man.
Oh, my swan, my drudge, my dear wild rose,
you tore down the bricks, the mortar, and the stone.
You threw away the whips, the shackles, and chains.
You planted your seed in the great barren land,
and we harvested, we harvested!

Early Thaw

You come
rushing down the mountain,
melting into my flowing stream,
beating yourself into foam
on the smooth rocks of my body.
You come and come until exhausted,
no longer struggle apart, but blend
as blood blends with water,
as our blood blends in orgasm.

Hunter

My stomach quivered like Jell-O
in a sea of rainbows
I reached to touch your back,
slid my fingers from neck to tip.
"You can't sleep," you said.
Put your hand on my body,
pressed fear into nowhere.

Let me go down on your carpet
of grass, your straw mattress.
The child in me is dying, dying
to be eaten like raw cattle,
a sweet meat fruit torn from wild
trees. I am not a street map.
You have found me, a virgin
in a thicket of thorns.

The hunter stalks with his tongue
the contours of my skin.
Each cell sparks then smolders,
and I burn; I burn the way
straw burns.

Knee Spot

Your kiss on the back of my knee
is a gypsy moth at my window,
the heat from my body drawn
to that dot, a little flame.
Oh, yes, yes, yes, my darling,
two little Zippos striking
there at the back of my knee, two
feather eyelashes
butterfly kissing, yes!
Oh, yes, yes, yes, building
a bonfire red, red, red.

Leaven

You fit into my sleeve,
the other half of my coat.
You fold me into your body,
knead me, knead me,
and I rise
slowly,
like warm bread.

Panther

Sleek black of his back,
warm in the sun
of the forest, laying.
She, frozen in her path,
poised to the scent,
he holds her.
Senses focus through
thick green underbrush,
leaves of the trees
are carriers of musk.
She waits.
He moves quickly, quietly
through the forest,
his body a symphony
in tune with the elements.
His great heart pounding,
he comes upon the clearing,
where she waits.
The ritual begins.

Playing to Win

I hold your face in my hands,
cup the smooth bones
of my bones.
I ache in the night;
secrets need telling.

I touch your feather lashes
with my tongue,
taste your full lips—
that smell of loving—
and whispered,
"I play to win."

I slip my hand over
your warm body
and beg to know the mind
that breathes beneath those lashes.
I shake you awake
with kisses. I cover you.
You rise to my touch.
We play to win.

Post-Script

Today I want you,
but you are gone.
I slip into a steaming
bath and rub hot lather
over my body, teasing it
into response. I lay on
the bed and massage scented oil
into my skin and place you there
beside me.

You take my breast between
your lips and caress the velvet
skin, abdomen, legs. Thighs open
and enter your hand, plunging deep
into me, clitoris swells beneath
my fingers—warm, wet, sweet.
You drink the nectar of my orgasm;
its heady scent intoxicates your brain.
We climb and climb to where no man has dared
and cry the tears of ecstasy.

Spider Woman

Your hand slips beneath
the black silk leg,
the pain of your emptiness
a ragged touch
of blood and passion
that traces my pelvic bone.
You press your hand hard,
hard into the mound
of black, soft curls.
Your mouth nuzzles into
my neck, burning itself
in dreams, kissing the
black silk breasts. Nipples
rise to peaks of softness.
You slide down me,
I pour myself onto you,
covering your body
with soft black silk.

Strangers

One hand touches;
one heart lightens
the burden carried
there.

Tears stain the face
one hand touches
away.

Softly, one hand
surrounds to meet
It's other, pressing
one face
close
to his chest.

Her wet lashes
make tiny roads
into his soul.

Poems of Therapy

The following are Poems I wrote while working as a Poetry Therapist at Rhode Island Hospital and as a visiting nurse in Providence, RI and Cape Cod.

Driver

Vibrating circles of light cut the night
left of yellow, searching for my eyes.
I would be taken. I could not escape,
drawn like a drunk to a drink.

Silence split the darkness like
blades of grass.
Film unraveled with horrific speed.
Backwards…Frame...god, help me…
…Frame…Frame…

Traveling nurse, dark time, undone
family waiting. Divine intervention.
Good Friday, it was. Pain punctuated.
Bodily functions switched off,
slowing, slower, slowed. STOP.

SMASH! Ripping steel like paper
crumpled for TRASH.
Light against light, throwing spears
into the air.
Bizarre. Still…the tinkle of glass.

Tiny breaths, pain, suffocating screams
in my head, tears in the air,
hanging like crystals, foretelling

NIGHTMARE. NIGHTMARE.

Body broken.
The pain seemed to blend
into nothingness,
where everything ends.

REVIEW SYSTEMS:
SHUTDOWN UNNECESSARY FUNCTIONS:
EMERGENCY SYSTEMS TAKE OVER:
FRAME: FRAME: ORDER:
ASSESS ENVIRONS:
ASCESS PAIN:
TRIAGE TO AUTO PILOT.

Killingly St…Providence, RI
Destiny or Decision?

*I was hit head-on by a drunk driver while working for the Providence VNA in 1993 working the 12-8 P.M. shift. It was at the end of my last client.

For Cynthia

A volunteer at McCauley House, Providence, RI
Published in the Journal of Art and Aesthetics in Nursing and, Health Sciences

I touch you, and I
have knelt to touch
the earth. Its warmth
rests in my palm.

You stand before me, holding
masses of children of this
time and future time.
You struggle to feed
each of them, not
letting one be hungry.

You are accountable to the
future, yet we fail to see
the significance of
bread and manna.

You dish up soup in the
kitchen of the poor, where
the hungry of Providence

line the walls in ribbons.
They come for food,
the hope that rises
from a job, love, and children.
The toothless come to McCauley house,
dunking their fresh bread in
thick, warm stew, wrapping coats and
shawls around empty bodies,
watching the hungry children and the
faces of the elders
etched in silence.

With hunger put away,
you walk among these people,
asking each his legend,
listening acutely for sounds
signaling despair.

At McCauley house
in Providence, Rhode Island,
special people keep
the world from dying,
the future from crying
and death from embracing all.

For Those That Have Left Me

There are ones I loved who have left me, left others that I love and now are in heaven where they look down on all of us .

Tara Marie

July 24, 1963 –June 8, 1985

Child of the wind,
you knocked at the door,
but it would not open.
The world would stay closed
and only now, in this moment
of death, would it embrace you.
We, the people of the world,
send you off knowing
that we offered all that could be given,
did what needed to be done.
In your wake lies a million
questions, unanswered as you
are unanswered, an unopened envelope
addressed now to God.

Safe Passage

For Nancy, April 13, 2009

Today, the rain. "Angels' tears," I said to you.
You smiled, knowing tomorrow
you would send the sun from
heaven to dry our tears.

Daughter, sister, wife, mother,
friend, guardian, my Captain!
Oh, how we will miss your spirit,
your gentle steerage through
oceans upon oceans of wild
and peaceful seas. Strong at
the helm, you were always
present for each of us
to throw a line and find safety
in your heart. We knew!

We thank you for allowing us
to be touched by your love,
to be sheltered by your kindness,
to be nurtured by your strength, and
to be guided by your wisdom.

Now your anchor to this earth is
hoisted, your sails are full, and
the great wind carries you off
and up to God. We will sail on,
stronger and with courage,
for we know that you will
always be there at the helm.
Captain of our ship,
we love you!

For Maryann

October 17th, 2017

A long time ago we wore white caps
White uniforms and white shoes,
We walked the halls with smiles
But sometimes sadness surrounded us.
You would grab my hand tug a bit
Then give me that smile..
The giggle you tried to hide
Made this life worthwhile.

Nurses, moms, wives of the fallen
We stood strong to watch them grow
Oh Maryann, I love you so
But now it is done, and you must go.
I will meet you in heaven someday
And we will hold hands again.
Friends forever as we said
So very long ago.

And when a dear friend lost his father..

The Builder

For David Okerlund
February 2016

You are a builder, someone who
can put things together and create new
beauty out of chaos. Never mind
how deep is the mud, how hot
the sun burning your brain
you tell yourself again and again
I can do this it's not too late.

Inside your heart there is pain
a life that will never be again
the man who loved you
Is now gone, and you must be
so terribly strong.

There are so many thoughts
that need to have answers
whirling in your head at night
keeps you awake while you fight
the confusion, the question
will everyone be all right?

Yes they will, for a life gone by
will always be with them,
And I know why!
Because love never dies,
It's always there
All we have to do is share!

The Man of Light

For Ron Rainone

You plant the seeds and watch them grow
Just like he did so long ago,
He struck your life with lightning force
You were his boy, there is no remorse.
For he nurtured you and all the others
Into great people, there are no druthers.
You take life by the hand
And lead the others to understand
What a strong and loving person he was,
Standing tall and teaching us because
He loved us so very much.
He is not gone but lives inside
All of us with growing pride, we will be
Tall as trees that stand forever on the edge of time,
A silent forest thick and strong. We will know
He is the one who sends the sun to sing and shine
Down upon us with strength and love.
We will forever bloom, knowing he watches from above.

Respectfully, in your sorrow.

And for the man I loved, a memory that lives on forever.

The Sea and Me

Remembering Jack August 2016

A long time ago when I was free
A man I loved showed me the sea,
He took me sailing in a wooden boat
And said, "here is how you float",

And we did, after patching and paint
He taught me to sail, no complaint
"Hold on you land lubber" was his cry
And I never never asked why.

For I trusted the captain of my ship
Trusted him to guide me without a slip.
But as you know, the sea can change
Without any warning and rearrange.

The hurricane came, the wind was strong
It ripped me apart; there was no song,
For there was no music for us to sing
But I was still hanging by a string.

The rope then broke and away I swam
To find out who I truly am.
But I had two anchors in my hand
To drop into the solid sand.

The captain had given me the gift of life
Two sons, my anchors without strife
We hung on to each other a lifetime of love
Blessed by him who lives above.

The Journey With My Boys

Over the years, my boys have always been there for me, through thick and thin when life was hard and when life was good, when happiness was there and when it was not. I owe my life to them, and as I get older I want them to know how much I love them.

These are some of the poems I wrote throughout the years.

Gratitude

For Joe my secret angel
and Elaine, his shining star.

Gratitude not just for what you do for me,
but who you are to each other, and to your families.
Life is not easy for anyone and relationships are even
harder, trying to understand others takes a gifted mind and
the neuro-dynamics that you have,
because you know that feelings come from the brain
and not the heart.
Your role is not light; you care for the older and the younger,
the past and the future.
This is what my gratitude is, for you, both and it is forever.

When my oldest son Joe first met his wife, I was thankful that he had found her

Love Is a Gift

To Joe & Elaine

They say that love is a gift,
but rarely do they know
that it starts inside of you
and then begins to grow.

Some of us have the will
and power to express,
but others crawl inside
themselves, hiding in the mess.

The two of you had the seed
buried in your heart,
needing one and another
so love could truly start!

Now you spread that joy around
to everyone you touch
to see, to feel, the love you
share, so very, very much.

I thank you for the gifts you give
to me, to us, to everyone!

A Thanksgiving Note

For My Son Joe

I thank you every time
I get a Pedi, Mani or haircut,
see a good movie, or fill up my car,
go to the market or take a train
I thank you every time again.

When I sleep in my warm cozy bed
and wake in the morning with nothing to dread
I gaze out the window and see the sun
and thank you every time my son.

A long time ago when life was so hard
I didn't know if I could be, the mom
you needed to help you grow
and raise your brother all in tow.

So scarred was I, full of anger and pain
no place to turn to stop the rain.
until you said, " it's all right mom, we'll find a way
if we hold hands we'll be ok."

You stood and watched your father die
holding our hands we all did cry
a life so wasted he never knew
how his children rose and grew.

And so my son, on this day
I give thanks in every way,
for my sons so strong and bright
I never have a dreadful night.

I know you will continue to live
your life with so much more to give,
I am so proud of who you are
my life, my love, my shining star!!

Always, With Love,
2015

Your Voice

For Elaine, September 2013

The world needs your voice it needs you to scream into the universe: HEAR ME!

It needs your heart to open telling secrets past so deep a river
running to the ocean will ebb and flow,
the sand and stone words will show you do not stand alone!

Your belief in what can be will change the world
for all to see,
others then will flock to hear, your words resounding in the air,
of healing, of happiness
and of joy!

So scream, my friend loud and clear!
the world is waiting for all to hear!

Elaine

From onset Mass.2003

How light his finger
touches your cheek
across your lips,
you close your eyes
and drift
into your soul.

Alone you speak
in silent whispers
descending into and
falling past the rags
of weeds and vines.

Down through the chaos
splattered lightening
fragmented thought
touching moments of clarity.

Softly resting final sand
sifting through fingers
reaching for reality

You

Rise

Strong

gathering self, learned
with unrelenting discovery
questioning, answering questions..

You Know!

How light the touch
that lifts the soul,
how warm the love
that fills the heart.

Elaine's Gift

This was a gift of a sculpture that is of a heart in two hands. The story went like this: there were two artists that created a single piece of art, then sent their piece to another artist that lived in Onset Massachusetts. He then created the sculpture of "a heart in hand". I found this sculpture and sent it to Elaine with the following note.

From Onset Cape Cod

Two individual artists in two separate
places each created a single piece.
It was an expression of their inner longing.
They both then sent their pieces to another artist
on a tiny island off Cape Cod.
When he received them both he studied their expression for a while,
looking at the delicate pure white hand reaching out with open palm,
and the smooth solid heart,
a red core surrounded by purple ribbons.
At once he knew they needed each other
and he placed his heart in her palm.
The two pieces drawn together it seemed, by love.
Let this sculpture always remind you of how you fit together.
Hold his heart gently in your palm, never closing over it,
always open to the universe and he will rest forever there.

The Seed

For Dr. Davey

A tree was planted long ago
In a forest full of shadow
It started out a little sprout
And then began to grow.

It struggled hard to find the sun
Through dirt and stones it came undone
A tiny twig with many arms could not
Dig through the earth, it hurt a lot.

The tree began to think, he didn't know
How difficult it was to grow
Through all the soil and the lime
To arrive at the sun in time.

He cried out for help, he wanted to be strong
Then a voice inside began a song
"You can be as tall as the trees, as strong as
The mountains, gentle as a spring breeze"

"You must believe in yourself".

So on he grew, the tiny twigs becoming one tree
He became one with the earth, one with the wind

And one with his spirit. He sheltered those who
Needed warmth, cared for those who cried in pain,
Healed those who could not grow by showing
Them how to say, "I believe in you"

The tree has grown strong and tall,
looking at the mountains
Feeling the wind in its leaves
Whispering Believe, Believe, Believe.

For My Davey

A rainy day full of gloom and wind
Descends upon us full of sorrow
We look to the sky for some change
Knowing it will come tomorrow.

It will come, we do know that
For mother doesn't wear a hat
But covers her beauty with a scarf
Shielding from the burning sun
Never leaving things undone.

The vines still cling to rocky walls
Undisturbed by wind or rain
But Spring will bring life again
Thankful for this nasty pain.

And so my son, just patient be
For your Spring is coming
Just wait and see
The flowers will bloom
The sun will shine
You will find peace,
Just give it time.

Life

For Joe, on his Birthday

Listening to the waves
Softly caressing the sand
Brings me the kind of peace
That you will understand.

As we get older day by day
We look back and silently say
What did I do, how was it done?
With your help, you were the one.

You will never understand that moment
Just taking my hand or smiling that smile
The one that is For me alone,
Like a queen, the highest throne.

To be your mother has been my pride
You capture all the good inside
And spread it all by holding hands
Leading me to safe dry land.

So life goes on, each day my son
Someday to be over, but remember this
You gave me the reason, you were the one
That taught me to love with a kiss.

So life will go on and who is to say
Where it will end some lovely day
I thank you for giving me purpose and drive
Knowing you were always by my side.

For Joe

You have reached half of your life
Some joy, some happiness and some strife.
What the future will bring is up to you.
Remember the past and explore the new.
Always keep close those you love
Sort of like a hand in glove.
So count your blessings every day
Love those that will always say
"I will guide you, give you the reason
Make your life good whatever the season".
And for the next fifty years, I will be near
My love will never disappear
Either by your side or from above
Know you always have my love.

Poems For Friends

These are poems for friends that have reached out to touch me and I hope they touch the hearts that I care for deeply.

Architect and friend who built me a wonderful home!

The Architect

For David Okerlund
Thank you for my home!

With the brush of a stroke
the spirit flows.
It dips and swirls,
painting your soul
upon a canvas,
parchment, paper,
wood, cement—
the stuff of earth.

Asking only
to feel your pneuma
to create your being,
to shelter your heart,
to wrap your spirit
in timelessness.

The pencil joins numbers,
fits curves and lines;
a notion binds itself to form
infinite possibilities.

Ruler directs the imagination
to bend a square,
to be different,
to be the same.

"There," he says. Out of the chaos
of mud and stone, wood and water,
arise infinite possibilities.
It is your cube, your magic space.
There is no darkness here,
but light and love, beauty,
peace, and safety.

To the right hand of my son Joe, and to my heart.

The Guardian

For Mary Lynn

An angel, a guide, a defender of good
a spirit of life so understood
sometimes the challenge is so hard
it cannot be seen on the card.
So on you dig deeper in order to find
what in the world is on his mind.

What makes you so strong, I really don't know
must be your spirit and rightly so,
ready to fix things in the flash of an eye
and never, never asking why.

I rest soundly in my bed at night
knowing you will shine the light
in the darkness to light the way
and everything will be OK.

Christmas 2015

To my physical mentor, the man who keeps me strong and has a heart of gold!

The Painter

For Jason

He looks at a white square
Thinks about color, texture and space
Closes his eyes and dives deep
Into his soul. The feeling then comes
Rising, rising into his mind as he
Dips the brush into the paint.

Where is my heart he says to himself,
It is here in my hand, but I want to see
The shape, the color with my eyes
I want to stop all those lies.

He touches the paint, takes the brush
Chooses the color, dips and swirls
Opens his heart that guides his hand
And creates a picture of his soul.

When all is done, he steps back
Looking at love not in black
But beautiful color that swirls around
The heart he painted that
Has no sound. Just lovely
Color for all to see, he painted
This wonderful heart for me.

Why Water?

For Michael Loffler

He plays with water
to see it flow
between the fingers
that somehow know
how it all started,
so long ago.

It dips and swirls with
infinite grace,
erasing past memories
that line his face.

He places his fingers in the pond.
The circles spread and grow
helping him to understand
what his little boat must know.

“You see,” he says, “I can control
the water as it comes
crushing down through dirt
and stone, powerful indeed!
It bends and blends and comes
to rest where I decided it should be.”

Water gives life, but takes away.
It hides itself or stands to say,
“I have stories beneath the clay.
The secret is to make me stay.”

No anchor for my little boat,
no rocks to lean upon.
I hid the story beneath the sea
and sailed on and on.

Why water? You ask, then I’ll tell you.
It brings me peace at night,
anchored by a little hand
the world is finally right!

Waiting For The Sun

For Michael Loffler

Blue sky, white puffs
Pass me by
White snow crystals
In my hands.

Where is the sun
don't understand
why it can't reach
my cold, cold hand.

Ever darkness
Ever dawn
Never leave
Lean upon.

Lost in mind
cannot see
door is closed
near to me.

Beckon you
shatter glass
shards of glitter
on the grass.

Surround the sea
Come to me.

Dig Deep

For Mike Monteforte

You harvest from the ocean
More than shells, but food
That feeds us in many ways
Brightening our dark days.

Water is your friend, the ocean
The pool, wherever you are
The water calls, you answer
And make it perfect again.

Thank you for your love of water

Eternal Question

For Marcia
In response to a lovely note you sent.

Two red flowers
Black stones beneath
You sent to me
A memory
Touched my heart
To remember
We are not free
Until we can see
The dark water
Upon which they lie,
Touch it make it move.

The question remains
What is the color of water?
How dense is the stone?
Life will go on
And someday see
We are together
You and me.
You are the water
I am the stone.

Who is the flower
Resting there?

The Gift

For My Sister Donna Louise

She sends a tulip in a tube
Held in wax
Stones of the earth
Blue bird of the sky
Sends it to me
From a name
I do not know

Is it you, my sister?
A greeting with no
Words, a wish for my
Birthday?
Where is the voice
I feel but cannot hear.

And if you try to speak
I will hear, for
Words are truly
All we have.

Vision Quest

For My Sister, Donna Louise

There is nothing to trust.
Necessary nothingness
that makes you trust
the minutes, the hours
that has borne you up till now.
Your life will flow again,
your children will bloom,
your sister will flower, and
your pain will bear fruit.
You will touch it
with your hand,
try it on,
see it fit like a glove.
You will lie in a wood of foxfire
and know at once exquisite pain;
to be able to love new,
you must be faithful
to the old.

Wait.
Even though you are tired
and the waiting seems endless,
you are not tired enough.
The music is near—

the music of children,
the music of sisters,
the music of pain;
you must hear it.
The music of your whole existence
echoes the mountain;
this is your reality,
learned from your sorrow,
and it beats you into exhaustion.

You Said To Me

For Linda

You said to me, it will be ok
I will see you another day
Something is in the wind
You must go where it calls
I can't come with you
It's not my place
But it will fill you full of grace.

So I left with your farewell
Not to journey down to hell
But to a place I know so well
Where women are healed and loved
Blessed by the God above.

I hear your voice in my head
Knowing I have nothing to dread
Think of a poem you said to me
It's in your heart for all to see.

Something Went Wrong

A memory

You are the needle stuck in his veins
Pushing despair into his soul
It is red like the color of blood
Drowning all self-control.

It feeds his anger and his rage
Pain consumes his every thought
It is long and complicated you have said
How about the day you wed?

Remember the words you spoke
That day not very long ago,
"I promise to be true to you
In good times and in bad,
In sickness and health,
Till death do us part"

Remember when you spoke those words
We watched as you both took that vow
A promise is forever, as we know
Please tell me that this is so,
Look deep into your soul and find
The lost love, you left behind.

Who Is There

Sitting by the great blue sea
High on a cliff looking down
Wondering if you called to me
From beneath the roaring sound
I'll never know who it is unless
I jump into the mess
Grab you by the foam
And bring you safely home.

I want you to be here with me
To wipe away the awful pain
That only we can see,
Come to me and explain
What it is that is that drives
You toward the deep dark sea.

The wind is whipping the ocean high
It is not your time to die
Reach out your hand, grab on to me
I will save you from the sea.

The Meaning of Life

For Joyce

Looking at you I see the beauty of life opening into your soul where the uncharted ocean lies.

I feel the current of which you yourself are unaware. If my mission is to touch your life as you have touched mine then it is also my mission to teach.

To lead you into your beautiful soul to chart for yourself
the virgin ocean of your depth of self-knowledge.
This is not a chance crossing we are upon it is a testing and teaching.

All that we are asked to do is to learn,
Each from the other, to unfold into greater beings
because we have touched each other's life.

This poem is for Joyce Hickey, when I started working at The Parkwood Hospital Psychiatric unit where she was the Director of Nursing. We had meetings every Thursday, and that was the beginning of our long and enduring relationship.

Thursday

For Joyce, 1990

To be given permission
for both sides of the brain
to grow at the same time,
creates a force of energy
that at once is powerful
and at the same time humbling.

One begins to know the feebleness
of the body,
As it struggles to match the energy
of the mind.

To create a middle ground for oneself
is impossible,
for to accomplish a task with mediocrity
is suicide.

When I give of myself, I become more,
for the sum of the whole is greater
than its parts, and experience is felt
as it is done.

The Joy of Sea

For Joy Sea

Whose boat am I
And who put me in the water
Who runs across my deck
I don't know why.

Sailing along I think of you
Boating on the calm, calm sea
You are The Who
I am the water

And we will be, what we will be
The boat on the ocean eternally.

And for my granddaughter Morgan who started writing and will continue on and on…

The Rose

For Morgan Rose Healey
May 2011

A seed floated
From heaven
Cradled in an angels
Wing, falling, falling

To the warm sand
Sinking deep kissed
By waves of love
Waiting for

The sun to smile
In a grandma's
Heart. The little
Seed began to
Sprout, slowly
Toward the sun.

It grew, and grew
And somehow knew
What it was looking for,

To blossom beauty
In our hearts and wrap
The world in love.

As grandma bent
To pick the rose
An angel said to her
NO, let me grow
And with your love
I'll bloom forever free

For Captain Bob who taught us about the big boat and all about life on the water.

Happy New Year

For Captain Bob

Once we sailed on the deep blue sea
Crashing through waves that were too deep
Be not afraid, hold the helm, hang on my friend
And listen to me

I am your Captain, I will teach you well
I will keep you from sailing into the swell
We will return home safe and sound
You will learn how to get aground.

I learned from my Captain more than this
He taught me to sail through life's misfits
Sometimes it's hard
Sometimes not so
Because you showed me
How to go.

Here's to you
And from my heart
I thank you forever
For helping me start

A life on the ocean, I love so much
And to always keep in touch.

Message In A Bottle

For Payton who found it.

There is a note in the bottle
I found down by the sea
Someone wants me to open
It traveled right to me
What is the message?
A secret, a story, or a key
I must open it just to see.

I pick up the bottle
But try as I might
I cannot open it
The cover is too tight.

So I sit on the ragged cliff
Holding the bottle
In my hands, wondering
Thinking, is it for me or
Someone who can't see
The message in the bottle
Resting on my knee.

I know it is a poem
I can see it through the glass
I must hold it tight
Then shatter it on the grass.

The bottle breaks, the poem
Falls to the soft green bed
I reach to touch it knowing
I have nothing to dread.

Why you ask...
The poem says..
I love you.
Come back to me.

Watching The Waves

Sitting by the great blue sea
High on a cliff looking down
Wondering if you called to me
From beneath the roaring sound,
I'll never know who it is unless
I jump into the mess
Grab you by the shining foam
And bring you safely to my home.

Time Will Tell

For Rick Gallos
My Financial Advisor

Life does have its twists and turns
You said to me and stay the course
I will keep you safe.
What do I say in response?
Hold tight, hang on, a wild ride
Is ahead but more for you than me
So I say..take a deep breath
And know you are loved.

A lovely lady said that to me
Many years ago, I read it every day
Looking at those words she wrote
She helps me carry
The burden of life
Helping others through their strife.

So my friend, close your eyes
And know the world is full of lies
But truth is in your soul
Only you have control
You will win, for me, for us all
You are too strong to take a fall

For Jon

Jon Kabat-Zinn, "Coming To Our Senses"

Lecture March 16, 2017, Brown University
Contemplative Studies

As I struggled to find myself I turned to poetry because as you said, "poetry has the potential to enhance our seeing, and even more importantly, our ability to feel the poignancy and relevance of our situations, our own psyches, and our own lives."

Poetry has helped me to look inside myself and see what is actually there. I sit on the sand; the ocean surrounds me, holding the stone I find my soul.

Respectfully, Tonia

Poetic Works From Morgan Healey

The following poems were written by my granddaughter Morgan Healey,

When she was in High School at Friends Seminary in NY. She was 14-16 years old and we communicated through poetry as we went on in life.

Morgan Healey
2/14/14

The Shape-shifter

If you are ever cold
I will be your sweater
Always keeping you warm
On nights you cannot weather

If you are ever falling
And somehow lose your grip
I will be your parachute
In case you ever trip

If you are ever tired
But can't sleep on your own
I will be your blanket
And you will never be alone

If you are ever a bird
Flying over the sea
I will be beside you
Together we will be free

And if you can't remember
How much you mean to me
I will remind you again
Until you can clearly see

If you ever need me
To fight troubles our world may bring
I will always shape-shift
For you I would be anything

Another new poem, Happy Valentines Day, love Morgan

A poem for Grandma

A woman floating on the sea the
waves brought her down
Resting, thinking, laying, questioning
Deciding to float or to drown
Life was hard and exhausting
and the water seemed so bright
What was stopping her from sinking
Becoming one with the eternal night?
She closed her eyes and held her breath
Ready to face her fate
The tide would take her wherever it went
Salvation seemed too late
But as she thought, still listening
a voice called out from afar
"Grandma, please, come back to me"
Words purely from the heart
The winds swirled and the waves collapsed
carrying her to the land
The girl's love had pushed her grandma home
now she could understand
Even though it may sometimes seem
like life is sinking you down
My love for you is as deep as the ocean
and I'll never let you drown

Happy 75th Birthday Grandma! I love you so much! Never forget how important you are to me.

Love,

The Youth of Our Nation

You cry for the youth of our nation
We hold out our hands, waiting for rain
We drown ourselves in your endless tears
For we are addicted to your pain
We, who are hopeless and reckless,
Always troubled, searching for signs
We shoot your bliss into our veins
Help us, guide us through this time.
You, who were meant to lead us
You, who will always deceive,
You, who have bloodily bore us
You break us, yet want us to achieve
Trace the footsteps, one by one
We follow the paths you have made
Hungry we are, for knowledge, for reason
To your orders, we always obey
You tell us "consume, never question"
You feed us tales of where we will go
We inhale sins in search of your heaven
You say we'll find it if we cherish you so
But the fruits you bore us were sour
And your paths gave us nowhere to hide
The footsteps you traced us have changed us
We're contorted and soulless inside
You cry for the youth of our nation
You mourn us and wonder how we died
Yes, you cry for the youth of our nation
But *you* are the reason that we're not alive

Paint

A frame of glass reflects a beautiful girl
Put together, no smudges, sharp edges
Posture straight and cheeks rosy
Smiling at all times
Eyes of water, clean and bright
Staring at the reflection
Paint on porcelain
(it can never chip)
(it will never chip)
Eyes of water, stormy seas
She is cracking deep inside
Eternal colors, but the canvas crumbles
(smile more, never break)
(no crying, the paint will run)
Coat more layers one by one
Never let them see
(who said beauty was pain?)
(beauty is *paint*)
(just a little more paint)
Pristine girl
Painted girl
Beautiful girl
(happy girl?)
(never)

.

Self Reflection

December 2016

I met a girl in a crystal window
Though I never meant to see her
(I usually avoid her)
I did not want to look her way
But my eyes dragged my mind to her figure
Full of wonder
I never like to look at her face
A puzzle of mismatched pieces
I don't like the crinkles below her eyes
The way her thighs touch
The texture of her hair
(I could not find much I liked)
But as I stared into her eyes
I saw the pain she carried
And I realized there was beauty there
For beyond the surface
shone a light so bright that
I cried when I
            opened my eyes
And I parted my lips and said
"I am learning to love you"
            She told me the same thing

The Meadow

10/26/16

there is a meadow that
lies deep in the wood
where darkness has not touched
and the light holds dear
to her heart

the sky carries a singing breeze
through the trees and
sometimes the wind gets caught
in the branches, though
never for long

bright sounds of laughter
and bliss are always heard
while children flit and play

and no one dares to stop and
listen to the cries of the
hungry
outside the field
while they feast on their
moment's delight

and no one dares to
open their eyes
to peer over the edge
of the bright green grass
for they
might trip on
the daisies and
fall

and if you ask a passerby
what the meadow is called
some say it's ignorance
some say it's paradise

The Big Dipper

November 2016

You once showed me the big dipper
And you shone under its light
We counted every star in the sky
You said "close your eyes, make a wish"
(I wished to be with you forever)
You told me you wished to have a star in your pocket
So you reached up and took one from the Heavens
Holding it in your hands while it glowed
        But it crumbled in your fingers and
sunk to the ground, now black
like the dirt under your fingernails
So you reached for another
with a fire in your eyes
I had never known
But that one crumbled too
so you grew angry and said they were yours
        You took all the stars from the sky
Until the Big Dipper was gone
and it was dark and I could no longer
feel you there
but I heard you weeping
for you wished for the light

Ode to a stranger

I see you
And you see me
I do not know who you are
I do not know where you have been
I might never know your name
Or smell the scent that brings you home
I may never know how you like your coffee or
If you lay awake at night like I do
I won't understand
What brought you to this moment
Or how you like your eggs on a Sunday morning
If your mind is on the ground right now
Or if it's up in the clouds
And when I look into your eyes
I do not know what they have seen
If they wander when you walk the earth
Singing of joy or hate silently
And I will never feel what you carry
The weight of the clothes on your back
I will never hear the demons in your mind
I will never know if you
feel alive
I may not know who you are
I do not know where you have been
But I know that
you are
And that is reason enough
to smile

Mothers Gift

1/13/17

When I was young, my mother said
“One day you’ll grow tall, little one
Your seed is planted in my flower bed
So never let your petals shed
Just remember to dance in the sun

So I clutched my petals with all my might
I danced among thorn bushes with care
Just like mother said, I held on tight
Kept my rosy blossoms always within sight
Watched them flit amongst the air

But often I would lose my way
Giving my petals to those who deceive
Tumbling into dark where there was no day
I watched my flower slowly decay
Until there was nothing left but dead leaves

While I no longer frolic among the sea
Or look out to a roseate sky
I cherish the gift mother gave to me
The power to exist; the power to be
As I live in each moment that passes by

Innocence

1/27/14

A tree with branches stretching out
A great field with endless grass
The meadow on ran forever
Sunshine that would always last

Daisies growing tall and strong

All smiling softly at me

Burning sand scorched the Earth

And overlapped with the sea
And as I walked on the cool dirt

And picked the roses pure and white
I looked across the meadow
And saw something clear and bright
Something I had never seen
A danger waiting to begin

Like a tether against a wall

My wonder pulled me in
He beckoned me with pleasure
A poison apple in disguise

The wind howled in warning

I tried to run and hide
But as I tried to flee my fears
Escape to the meadow I knew
Things were changing all too fast
A new person was in my shoes
Time was running out so soon
The daisies were all gone
Like sickly poison in the air

The birds stopped with their song
I came to the Meadow's end
And realized something was wrong
I looked around and softly wept
For the meadow I knew was gone

Free

2/3/14

An unknown world never seen
The barriers were broken
Different shapes and meanings
Nothing needed to be spoken
The walls collapsed without sound
A brand new life without sorrow
The weights were uplifted
And there was a new tomorrow

Box of Crayons

2/12/17

Hush
Never disturb the restful
Let them remain full of wonder
I wonder if we are born with our eyes open
Or if someone closes them
Do they pinch them shut?
fingertips on infant eyelids
or do we know
to
Never open our eyes
For painted dreams do not carry over
into the reality of a sullen world
Unless we color it ourselves

Forever

1/20/14

The wind danced shyly amongst the trees

Whispering softly
Caressing her face
Her fears were taken away
The sun took away the darkness
An eternal light in a world of fear

The snow crunched beneath her feet like glass
A white blanket against the ground

It softly touched the branches and said hello
Then floated to the ground
Landing daintily on her shoulders
The river ran gently

Bubbling softly
As she walked by
Flowing and floating

Then retreating to the lake
Like a mother returning to her cubs
Holding them forever
The flowers grew strong on the branches

Parting in her favor
Untouched by the chill

Growing strong
The white clouds settled over the sun
And the pale moon peeked over the stars
Like a child afraid of the dark

The bluebirds sang
Their eternal song
Only for her
She laid her head on the soft snow
With rosy cheeks from nature's cold kiss
And picked the petals from the flower
As she settled down
And laid there
A flower becoming one with the snow
The echoes of the earth surrounded her
And she smiled

Thoughts on a sullen day

I was thinking about
Shiny things
Brilliant spaces
What it'd feel like to fall
I was thinking about
The dawn of the darkness
The ark of magnificence
The art of all
For I was thinking about
How I was thinking about
Nothing at all
The whiteness of creativity
Paint of the public
Fills the corners of the mind
No room for thought
And spreads itself
What shade is yours?
I will change
I will change

A Universe of Love

2/8/14

The world could stop spinning on and on
Frowning upon the stars

But as long as I have you in my life
Those problems seem so small.

The sea can break beneath my feet
Like an earthquake at it's peak
But as long as you are beside me
I have no worries at all.

Buildings could come crashing down
And everything could change
But we are carved on the wall
And we will stay the same.

The moon and the earth could collide
Like two sides at war
But you are my eternal peace
Our empire of love can never fall.

As the years pass us by
And many things come and go
Although things may change around us
Our love will stay the same.

Ode to 365

Wow. You've been tough. As you slip away, I can't say that I'm sad to see you go. I'd like to think that in your exit, you'll take all the hardships you've imposed upon me with you. That a new breath of life will suddenly fill me when you're gone, and suddenly I'll have the answer to all the problems you've left in your wake. But I know this could never be true. I will face the same challenges tomorrow that I face today, and your absence cannot take them away. Yet as I face the uncertain future, I can't help but reflect on the past. All the times you've made me cry, all the times you've tested me. The times you've left me helpless in situations I could not control, or left me gawking at how ruthless you can be. But in these times, you have brought me new moments too. New connections, passions, and a new appreciation for life itself. You've shown me joy in places I never saw before, because perhaps I forgot to look. And above all, you have brought me closer to the person I want to be, striving for a world in which I would like to live in. So even though you are coming to a close, I know your remnants will remain. They can be heard in my every word, and seen in the person you have shaped me to become. A person who you have shown me to love. And because of this, my final words are these:

Thank you.

Morgan Healey

Poetry Asks A Question

Poetry asks a question and some have answered. This poem I received from a woman who wrote back to me after reading Sand Stone.

Where Does Love Go

It is like a snail climbing up a beautiful plant,
slowly eating away the life of the plant until
there is no longer anything left.
It is very slow and devastating.

I had 3 beautiful baby boys in 3 1/2 years,
But now I am being reminded each day that I am worthless.
Why is the house not clean, why is the laundry not done
why is my dinner not cooked what do you do all day?

A constant reminder that the monster is the provider
and that I don't contribute.
My mantra is take care of my children.
The 3 boys and I go to bed early to escape the monster;
we read books aloud until the beautiful boys fall asleep.
I put the innocent boys to bed and get into my own
hoping to fall asleep before the monster returns.

This does not work the monster does not care that I am asleep
he has sex with me while I lay there numb and not responding
it does not seem to matter to him. I am not facing him but on
my side crying.

On another day, it is almost 5:00 pm I know the monster will
be home soon,
my stomach is in knots wondering what he will find that I did
wrong today.

I smile for my boys as I sit at the table feeding them dinner we laugh.
The monster comes in the house and the laughing stops.

I am in a very deep dark hole that I cannot seem to crawl out of
I think that it would be easier to just stay here
and wish the world goodbye
then I look at my beautiful sleeping boys and repeat my mantra
I have to take care of my boys.

I try and please the monster but nothing I do is right,
you did that wrong ,why are you so stupid?
I stop trying. never is it physical abuse but verbal and mental
I think this is worse it hurts to your core.

It is such a happy house full of laughter and fun when the
monster is not here, why does he have to keep coming home?
The boys are getting older and now finding ways to stand up
to the monster,
he is losing control, and it is now four against one.

The monster has now moved to the basement.
Unlike the monster under your bed
he does not easily terrorize us but he is still here
making us live on pins and needles.

We are getting stronger and we will fight this monster!

As to my question where does love go,

it is a slow process that sneaks up on you over time
and before you know it you are numb.
I know what love is by just looking in my children's eyes
and I hope that I will find it again, unlike the snail eating a beautiful plant
I want to be the butterfly that sits atop the plant looking down
and says life is good. I am on my way

Keeping strong Eleanor

And Finally To Listen

Listen

March 2011

And then he said; the past will be still
You will live only in today.
You are the stronger of all the others
Who were your life, helped you
Shielded you, taught you to love.

And when the self briefly dissolves
Out of the constraints of causation and
Locale what does it matter who is
Speaking..the wish for order
For form not in alignment

Disrupts the degradation of choice
Allowing the experience of voice
My own most insuperable possibility
The possibility of freedom.

Hear Me

Can you hear me
Crying in the dark
Face in a pillow
No one can see.

You are near
I hear a voice
Calling out
I have no choice.

There is a light
Beyond this bed
I must follow the beam
Or I am dead.

Listen listen quietly
Come to my room
And you will see
Someone who needs you
Speak to me.

I will listen to what you say
And hope for a better day.

Sunset Off the Cape

Winner New Yorker poetry Challenge 1979
Published in Issues magazine

She stood in darkness,
Against winters forbidding light.
Body of child soul of woman the sorrow
Of stone hung around her head like an *Albatross*,

And like the mariner who shot the pious bird
She too was cursed and murmured low,
mea-culpa mea-culpa mea-maximum-culpa
I am now alone, forever alone.

The faint music of Neptune's' guardians,
Danced on the shimmering bay,
And held her senses taught with excitement;
I will soon join my love
I will soon be free-
Free in death.

She had been beaten down by the coastline,
Formed and reformed as if some giant fist
Pounded her life into gravel and sand
Oh she loved him with unchecked passion
And she died as if by his hand.

At dusk her life was scattered leaves,
And strewn upon the waves;
Twice surrendered she.

You too, sing America

Yet you don't seem to see
Not everyone is happy, not everyone is free.
The carpenter, the mason, the shoemaker all sing
Never truly looking, at what they're worshipping.

Sing America! Sing it blithe and strong!
But never will I sing it, 'til it be restrung.
The foundation is built on oppression,
Yet no one seems to put into question

Why sing America?

Land of the Free? Home of the brave!
More accurately - home to the ones who crave
Money, power, greed, fame.

Let us be the new United States,
And let us act and govern with love, not hate.
I assure you, we will then live in a democracy,
We will then live by the laws of liberty.

We too will sing America.

Joey Healey
January 22 2019

Acknowledgements:

Inspired by Langston Hughes, "I Too Sing America"

I would again like to thank all those who helped me with editing, organization and comments on my book.

Dr Jay Korsen, DC, Chiropractor, Author and Friend
David Okerlund, Architect and Friend
Joyce Hickey, PhD, RN, APRN, Best Friend
Joseph Healey, Son
Morgan Healey, Brown undergraduate, Granddaughter
Thank you for your poems

If we can do nothing else, we must listen.

Note From David Okerlund

"Scripture says that wisdom is as old as creation. That wisdom was the breath of God. It is embedded in all that ever has been or ever will be created. The chaos of being human keeps us from seeing it. But some, like artists (poets) and prophets can see through the chaos and describe for us a truth that is hard for the rest of us to see. Artists invite us into the sacred space of creation -- a place of grace and discovery. This is the place where wisdom is revealed. When we experience the work of the artist, sometimes it resonates with us and in that moment the chaos disappears and there is a truth revealed about living, or dying, or loving. I think your book is the gift of wisdom. Not so much your story this time, but the revelation of a lifetime of learning, shared through the created word so that others might be changed. The collection of poems for and to family and friends made this crystal clear. This is a special person showering those she loves with the wisdom that could only come from the life she has lived. "

Tonia Teresa Healey is a retired Psychiatric Nurse, living in Narragansett, RI. She is a certified Poetry Therapist of the National Association of Poetry Therapy. After becoming a nurse she attended Brown University where she did an Independent Concentration, titled Poetry as a Therapeutic Process. She is also an "Army Brat" growing up all over the world with her Dad. She has written a previous book "Sand Stone," and published many poems.